Living Togeth
Killing Each other

Mine, OURS and Yours

Teresa Karlinski

t.a.k. cat Publishing

ISBN: 9798773293200

Cover by Teresa Karlinski
Images by Canva

An Intergenerational Household Survival Guide: 2
Living Together Without Killing Each Other

Mine, OURS, and Yours

CONTENTS

I dedicate this book to my daughter Laura and granddaughters, Hanna and Lillian. Thank you for being interested.

JOINING HOUSEHOLDS

Separate or on one floor?

EARLIER, IN BOOK 1, we looked at the various combinations of living arrangements. Honest discussions will help create a middle ground for everyone. This is a family affair, after all. My effort here is not to dissuade your move forward but to point out the limitations and adjustments during your planning. I had conversations with families I know who had also gone through this process. To these, I added my experience. The aim is to break everything down into manageable bite-size pieces. Some points may sound trivial or too easy. But believe me, life is life and full of unexpected hurdles.

Enormous sacrifices will end up as grudges and you know how they fester over time. Be good to yourself. Don't put yourself last, no matter if you are a young spouse or grandparent. The whole point is to meld together into one big, happy family.

The first few days and weeks, we each settled in, but soon I realized nothing I said counted for anything. To keep the peace, I bit my lip.

Furniture

It makes sense, doesn't it, to assess how much furniture everyone owns which fits into your new house? It's hard parting with favourite pieces if you must if it cannot fit into the house.

Should your new home offer two floors and a finished basement, this provides more space and privacy. It could be the old ratty couch has seen better days, and it's time for a love seat for your room if you don't occupy your own separate living area.

If the house is large enough, you may find room for all or most of what filled your previous individual houses. Familiar surroundings are always a comfort, and you deserve it, right? True, if your bedroom is your only private space, only so much will fit in there. In other areas, either the attic (if you have one) or the finished rec room, you can furnish with an assortment of everyone's pieces.

Your previous furniture may not suit the style of house you now live in. If small children live with you, you might not wish your new anything out where the little ones can 'age' the furniture before its time. Sharing is caring, as the saying goes, and if worse comes to worst, cover that new piece and smile.

I had a whole finished basement to myself, where I updated a basic summer kitchen and had room for most of my previous furniture.

Keep it simple

Early communication is extremely important. If something annoys anyone, you must attempt to clear the air, otherwise, you can expect friction and failure from your shared living experience.

It is helpful to hold monthly (or otherwise) family meetings regularly where individuals can vent their frustrations. (See Communication: How to conduct a family meeting)

Scheduled meetings take the heat out of the moment but allow for proper communication. When an individual is too hot-under-the-collar to handle an immediate complaint and must wait for the next meeting on the calendar, their anger cools and distancing from their immediate irritation assures a more satisfying discussion.

Minute-taking during meetings will quell recurring situations from being repeated over again.

Forewarned is forearmed. It's best to nip problems in the bud.

I hadn't considered some of the following situations before our move. Though I thought I'd done my homework, they required careful and specific deliberation earlier. I started the first meeting, but bored glares and deaf ears met me across the table. By not dealing with minor problems early, we experienced angry silences and stiff chins. Listening, negotiating, sharing respect are magic tools.

Sometimes, timing is everything—yours and the rest of the family. Why deal with hindrances? This is your life. How tightly do you want to trim the deal? How much are you willing to choke grievances down? Why should you anyway? Why should anyone?

Because you're such an old softie, an easy-going person, and a fabulous mother-in-law/father-in-law, don't suppress your needs only to keep the peace. If you do it enough times, you'll feel like an underdog! Better to get everything out in the open early.

Oh yes, remember who has seniority, not to mention that little title on the mortgage called major shareholder if that is you? What are you going to do when things don't work out? Move? Not likely.

Communication

MY FAVOURITE MANTRA IS: It is much easier to start out with tight rules and loosen them than to tighten loose ones.

Because life is a family affair and the more family members or friends included in the home, meetings may well be a lifesaver. Pick a time and day—let's say the first of the month or the first Friday or whatever day and time the whole family is free to attend.

Instead of dealing with an issue in the heat of the moment, you wait for the regular meeting, whether the wait is a week, a day, or weeks. Discussions work best when everyone has a cool head.

Take minutes to keep a record so there is no mistake what everyone agreed to, by whom, and who not.

How to conduct a family meeting ☺

You've been at work all day, stuck in a couple of meetings, and here's a suggestion for another one at home. The reality is they work. At least at home. The bigger the family, with or without added friends, meetings may well be a godsend. Should an emergency arise, by all means, call everyone together as soon as possible. Otherwise, save a regular day and time.

About meetings

Who will be the moderator? (Head of the household /patriarch/matriarch, the same person or, to be inclusive, will people take turns?)

This person will keep the meeting moving forward smoothly and exercise veto power when/if necessary. Any speaker is the keeper of the talking stick till he or she finishes and passes it to the next person.

A fun family activity in preparation

What is a talking stick? Based on the age of the children, you might suggest they decorate the talking stick. This is a dowel, or a clean, dried tree branch embellished however you or your children's imaginations take them.

The person speaking in the meeting holds it to remind everyone to be quiet and hear them out. They then hand it to the next speaker or set it on a table in the middle of the meeting circle if you are not following an agenda or are holding an informal meeting.

YouTube has several examples you may adapt as your own or change up. Conditional to the age of the children, they may need supervision while doing this craft. Don't be surprised how they throw themselves into the creative process. Afterward, they will feel a vested interest in the meetings.

My simple and favourite talking stick is a long pencil painted with water-thinned glue and rolled in glitter. Just an idea young children might adopt.

I hadn't heard of the talking stick at the time we made our move and the children were too young to decorate one. I love this idea.

Why family meetings?

Even a married couple making plans needs a discussion about wants, essentials, necessary strategies, etc. Everyone wants to be included in whatever will affect them. Reasons for getting your group together are varied, interesting, and informational. The following are a few ideas for you to expand on.

- To plan family outings, vacations, air grievances, discuss routines, set up work schedules, etc.

- For a sense of togetherness and accomplishment

- To make transitions smoother: new arrival, a pet passing, a new pet

- To reinforce family values

- To share information

- To celebrate achievements, a job situation, health issues, etc.

- Each person speaks from youngest to oldest

- Take minutes and check none are missed before the meeting is over

- You should follow specific rules of the meeting for consistency

- For everyone's accountability in the household

- All attendees might sign the minutes upon reading them when they become public (shortly after the meeting)

- To note absentees

- File minutes

- No hot-headed discussions allowed. Everyone must stay calm.

Successful meetings

The secret is to begin on a positive note to relax your fold: tell a funny story or a joke even the children might enjoy. Or not. You know what works for your gang. Some points to take into account:

- Keep meeting upbeat (discuss good/enjoyable things first)
- Assess how everyone is doing
- Find a time that works best for everyone overall
- Plan on a consistent day of the month and time
- The first couple of meetings may be disorganized till you work out a routine
- Use "I" messages
- Solve one problem at a time
- Keep meetings short (we all hate meetings and children get bored)
- Everyone listens without interruption
- Establish a time limit for each speaker
- Rotate meeting responsibilities (meeting coordinator, secretary, timekeeper)
- Make decisions by consensus

- Mom/Dad/Patriarch/Matriarch (mediator) has veto power

- The benefits of family meetings are the same as successful meetings

- No member can attend if not calm

Post a page in a central area of the house—probably the fridge in the kitchen—so everyone can add grievances or other topics for discussion to the agenda all month before the meeting

No one needs to sign their name to the agenda items they add

A list of discussion items helps the meeting coordinator consider how much time to plan for and how younger children will be entertained so they don't fuss

An emergency meeting may be necessary due to urgency or time constraints

Hot water use

With many individuals under one roof and dependent on the number of bathrooms and/or showers, scheduling bath time is a necessity according to your situation. More or less. Some family members may become disgruntled when scheduled times are not convenient because of last-minute circumstances. What would you suggest as a solution? Here's where a discussion and vote by consensus come in handy.

The water tank capacity is also a factor as only so many showers in a row will be hot. Add to that a certain amount of time in there. Your days of a lo-o-ng hot shower are over unless you're home alone one day. Smile.

What rules do you encourage or discourage? How will you handle resentful individuals? Just keep it simple.

Temperature control

Who has access to the thermostat? I'm serious. Please don't say, everyone. Do you need a lockbox on it? Should only one temperature be constant? Who is in charge? More arguments happen over temperature than is obvious. You bet it happens.

If a family lives in the basement and you possess one thermostat upstairs, remember heat rises and the downstairs does not benefit. Are the walls properly insulated in the basement? Is it possible to install a fireplace insert?

If the people on the first floor complain using the fireplace raises the temperature on their floor, what's the simple solution? Think. How about turning down the temperature upstairs so everyone is happy? Easy-peasy? ☺

Dealing with broken rules

In every family, someone disrupts the status quo now or then. Mistakes, forgetfulness, self-centredness happen. Clear rules make for a happy home. The more people in a household make it harder to overlook transgressions that affect the well-being of the entire household.

As always, your family meeting is your friend. How urgent is it you arrange one right away? Have you consequences for misbehaviours discussed from an initial family meeting before setting up house? Depending on the wrongdoing, how tough are you willing to get? How many offences can one person get forgiven before the bottom line and 'here's your hat, what's your hurry' is invoked by consensus? Remember a family vote works better than one person lowering the boom.

HOUSEHOLD BILLS

YOU DISCUSSED HOW TO divvy up bills and expenses to everyone's satisfaction before moving, right? This is more important than you might consider at first.

Who will contribute to the higher bills like house insurance and property taxes, for example? How? By deposit to a household bank account at a specified time before the bill comes due?

You don't want misunderstandings or re-negotiating changes after everyone has agreed during your family meeting. Sometimes, an unhappy individual may cause strife because they are not holding up their end by being contrary, disorganized, or late with payments. Better yet, when you took minutes and had all discussions as proof in black and white, no one should argue. Minute-taking is a lifesaver and great mediator.

Groceries

If there is one kitchen and individuals take turns cooking, doesn't it sound fair you contribute equally to a grocery jar unless either children or adults experience certain food restrictions? If only one person likes a certain food, should you penalize everyone to pay for it? This is no reason to nitpick since it's only one food. Let's assume a member hates steak or chicken or fish, or is vegan or a vegetarian? Discuss how to handle this beforehand.

It seems fair you give individuals with certain likes and dislikes a free pass unless you catch them eating your leftovers from the fridge which would cross the line. It happens—don't laugh. Do you feel a family meeting coming on?

Should the recreation room provide a summer kitchen and the grandparents, or another family combination, enjoy their space there, all should agree or disagree if everyone eats all meals with the family or if grandma cooks for her and grandpa. In that case, they pay for their own groceries and what-not if they are not sharing with the rest of the family. Although at least one meal a week together—somewhat of a potluck—is a wonderful excuse for togetherness.

In our situation, we shared a family dinner once a week. We voted on the night most convenient for members free from countless outside interests and schedules. This is a perfect opportunity to share each other's past week and enjoy some closeness if life is super busy.

Detergent

Detergent is one thing people might take turns buying at a place like Costco so everyone may share or not. It's your family; you get to decide. No one can make you do anything. There are no hard and fast rules, only family rules. Consider buying food and necessary household items in bulk when you can if you've enough storage space.

Indoor expenses

Who will be the overseer of preventative upkeep, maintenance, and repairs? Just like having individual homes, care of all working parts inside the home requires regular attention.

- Major appliances - fridge, stove, dishwasher
- Built-in microwave
- Toaster, toaster oven, air fryer, etc.
- Furnace (filter changes)
- Water tank

- Plumbing

Internet, cable, streaming services

The sad fact is none of us can avoid the internet. Doesn't everything you do happen there? Do you shop, pay bills, attend on-again-off-again school classes, webinars, YouTube (promoting various how-to subjects) and so on. Who will pay for this and how?

What about streaming services? Do gamers live in the house? Would a second internet account help if gaming is a big thing for the families to prevent Wi-Fi interruption or overload reliance on your service provider, where you live, and the number of people using it at the same time? Do you run a side business online? Would the families gain from individual accounts and pay for their own bandwidth? Probably. Grandma and Grandpa are likely not heavy users and won't need their own accounts. Or maybe they do. Every household is different. ☺

Are you still paying for cable? Another discussion may be necessary. Nowadays, how much do you watch it with all the streaming services on offer?

Unique personal items - cell phone or other individual services

Should personal items used solely by one person and owned by them before the move remain their expense? Cell plans differ, as do persons who buy them.

You can save a bundle of money for the household. Try a plan all users can get what they need or as close as you can. Even youngsters and especially teens possess phones these days. Family plans are great regulated by how many members the provider allows in a package. Check with your provider; you'll want to shop around for the best deal.

Divide the cost among the owners. Each cell owner deposits the amount into a household account. If anyone doesn't pay on time, or finds excuses not to, they get one warning or one more chance and if it happens again, they're on their own. The deal is to help each other, not drag down the rest of the group.

Upkeep and Maintenance of Building

JUST AS THE RESPONSIBILITY and maintenance of your single-family home needed attention, this house is no different. Will you use a slide rule of who pays how much according to the percentage of individual dollar investment in the house purchase? This is tough, but again, cool heads before the move deliberated who pays for what, why, how and how much. Right?

No one can tell you how to manage these expenses, but again, this is up to you to write your own rulebook. Minutes taken at a family meeting will keep everyone on an even keel and the particulars clear.

My son-in-law had no intention of being bossed by a woman. Surrounded by females, he was the man of the house and did everything his way. I made the mistake of suggesting a time-saver or a simpler way of doing an outside task, and he huffed and grumbled. Because we had no discussion about upkeep, maintenance, or preferences before our move, it was too late to make a big deal of it. He avoided me for days, and not wishing to stir the hornet's nest, I had to choke down my displeasure.

Outside expenses

- Driveway repair
- Roof
- Windows
- Garage door repair, inside maintenance
- Fence
- Deck
- Pergola
- Landscaping
- Repairs/upgrading our space

Outdoor Tools

Both (or all) generations joining the household can compare lists of tools necessary for the house. Separate a complete set to keep; you only need one. For example, unless you plan huge backyard gatherings, how many barbecues do you need or can store?

What do you need?

Once you sort through individuals' tools, you may scratch your head about an overabundance.

- BBQ
- Snow shovel or snowblower
- Garden tools: rake, lawnmower
- Spade if gardening
- Rake and hoe
- Garden shears
- Grass trimmer
- Watering gear/water hose
- Garden gloves
- Pruners according to your type of garden
- Wheelbarrow

When we (my daughter's family and I) bought a house together, her husband had two barbecues and though we were a family of three adults, a baby and a toddler, he couldn't part with them. I also had one but knew not to bring it.

Having had a house each to maintain, we had two sets of various garden tools. I left most of mine behind for the buyer of my house, as he'd sold everything before coming across the country with his family until they bought my house and settled in.

Had we not purchased a house with a double garage and not had a ready shed that came with the house, my son-in-law would lack enough storage space. Shortly after we moved in, he bought an additional small storage shed for all his stuff. Do you get the idea he was a packrat? Do you want/need extraneous tools taking up space, some are rarely used or not but cause clutter.

Gardening

EITHER YOU HAVE A green thumb, or you don't. It's only fair the person with a passion for gardening continues to enjoy enhancing the outside of your house. It might even be several people who enjoy varying segments of the work. It's a win-win for everyone. You end up with fabulous curb appeal and everyone's pride and joy.

How do you negotiate changes to the household (i.e. gardening, trees – what stays, what goes?)

Does everyone care about landscaping?

What kind of changes will the family unit hate? Whoever is in charge of the outside work—be it an individual, alternating person, or a team—might consider discussions at a family meeting. There's one on the calendar every month, same day and time. A vote is good only if this is a problem.

Examples of pitfalls/benefits

- Differences of opinion, style, experience might lead to locking of horns
- Once choices are made, what would be an important enough reason to rehash an agreement about yard work?
- Whoever has done the work has his say
- Is it worth fighting over maintenance of the yard?
- Decide who wants to be the man of the house (or woman)
- It's comforting to be organized

Cars, Parking, Transportation

Cars, car insurance, fuel

CARS ARE AN EXPENSE individual owners will probably be responsible for. Car insurance, maintenance, license renewal, and filling the tank belong with the car.

Let's say a member of the family doesn't drive, isn't licensed, or cannot drive because of physical disability? In the event, that person(s) needs transportation regularly and no local bus service is available, how will you handle this? Will they reimburse the car owner for gas or maintenance? Only you can negotiate an arrangement you are both/all comfortable with. Just a thought, but especially important if it's an ongoing situation.

Parking

Does your property allow parking for all cars in the household? Neighbours don't mind complaining if you inconvenience them or they don't like cars on the street in front of their house. These days everyone wants their own car since all family members are on different schedules and work in various locations.

To declutter the driveway, if you own a garage, park inside to lessen the wrecker's yard look in front of your house. The problem with this is whoever has dibs for inside parking will then play musical cars when they need to leave. Here's another aspect regarding imposition to others to chew over. It may be a good idea to suggest Grandma or Grandpa park inside. It depends on how socially active they are and whether parking inside or out would be more agreeable to them.

Visitors Parking in your Space

Either your driveway is plugged up with the household cars or someone's left on an errand and their regular access is gone due to visitors dropping by.

To keep the peace, be kind and ask visitors to park on the street or elsewhere. They are only around for a few hours and it's not fair that older members of the family should be inconvenienced because of your visitors hogging their spots or access to the garage if that's in question.

What about visitors in general?

Since several family members with cars live in one house, visitors should park on the street. Period. You don't want to box in a family member not joining in the entertainment and ask them to knock and beg to move a car. I can't think of anyone who enjoys musical cars. Can you?

In my wildest dreams, I could not imagine the nuisance and disruption parking might create. We had a two-door garage and two households. How could this be problematic? The answer is three vehicles: his, hers, and mine, with only two who might access escape at a moment's notice. Someone will be stuck waiting for someone else to move their car for a third person's exit. Remember, three into two doesn't go, even with today's mysterious math.

How many cars fit in the driveway?

Ha, that's easy. If need becomes a must, six cars fit in our driveway: three across with tight exits in and out of the cars and a second row behind that. Usually, this only occurred during a family party with no street parking available in the near vicinity. Only one person trusted himself to attend to this careful parking— my son-in-law.

Other than visitors, parking isn't a problem, right?

Too many times, moving cars out and in again is disruptive and tedious. It's like musical chairs, but after a while, it's not enjoyable anymore. Some days, you merely convinced yourself it's another opportunity to save gas by doubling up errands on another day, although it's inconvenient and feels constricting. It felt good when you found a silver lining, but as you became older, patience grew thinner. These types of impositions are frustrating and stressful.

YOUR SPACE AND MY SPACE

HURRAY. YOU'VE COME A long way and completed a lot of work collectively. Whether you choose togetherness as one unit, sharing one kitchen, laundry room, living room, etc. or any of the other possibilities, each will present unique situations.

Respecting privacy

Where do you draw the line? Think of it as your space and my space. Separate but equal.

This all depends on your living arrangement. If you have a separate entrance, chances are your quarters are separate, although you might share one common entrance and still maintain separate digs. If you live in the basement, you might come in through the front door or through the garage. If you're parked in there, and live in the basement, you don't need to bother with the front door. Sometimes, too many comings and goings are intrusive to the people on the main floor. Everybody's busy and may not wish added interruptions unless awaiting your arrival.

Do you want to stop and chat on your way in, or are you in a hurry? No, you're not anti-social. On the occasion you're carrying gifts for upcoming events, you want to keep them a surprise. You'd like to keep them under wraps, so you hurry to your room.

Upstairs/downstairs

You agreed individual families enjoy their own interests, schedules, priorities, etc. To not interrupt at awkward times, you agreed not to just walk in on a possible serious conversation, argument, or child's lesson or reprimand. You all have telephones and agreed to phone ahead. Try as you will, it won't always be a successful way of contacting a specific family member because they ignore their phone calls.

It's a good idea to decide how you will handle entrance/exit early in the game.

If you live in the basement and plan to entertain guests, do ask them to come in the front door, not through the garage. You might even install a doorbell at the front door for downstairs.

Try to make your lives as separate as possible, though still together. If you lived across the street, next door, or across town, you would need to telephone to ask a question, wouldn't you? Would you run into your relative's house instead of calling first? Could be yes or could be no. It depends on your family habits or culture. Picking up the telephone may be your first impulse. Ditto if you wish to share something. Phone if you wish to change the time for weekly Sunday dinners or if you wish to borrow a cup of sugar. The less intrusion, the better for everyone. The household has enough going on.

What if more family moves in?

The more family members or needy friends move in, someone must be in control to keep new arrivals appraised of expectations. Will they pay rent? What are the house rules? If early communication fails, is a Plan B ready to keep the peace with so many people in your house? Any number over five is harder to keep happy. Everyone should cooperate with the family's best interests at heart. That's your family, right?

Should your house operate like Grand Central Station, might handy pre-written house rules be available for new arrivals? Early instruction at the get-go leaves no leeway for misinterpretation.

Keeping Your Things Your things

Let's face it, items go missing, get misplaced, or borrowed by accident or not. Children like shiny things, interesting novelties. With less personal space, you may have forgotten some item in the bathroom when you showered or shaved. Then again, likely a family member thought it wouldn't hurt to use your deodorant since they're in the right place and the right time and they forgot theirs. Some people pick up items, not theirs, and forget to return them or their fingers are sticky. Be kind. Respect others' possessions, be they small or large.

You may wonder what's the big deal since you are all family. To be fair, if you lived next door or across the street, would you walk into the family home and help yourself to what doesn't belong to you because you need it? How much would it hurt if someone helped themselves to your things? See how that works?

How's Your Credit?

Have you heard you should never enter into money dealings with friends or family? It's hard to work out a plan on the spot when someone is in dire straits. Don't wait long to work one out. Before money changes hands is the ideal time. Work out a budget if the borrower isn't organized. Create a written agreement with a payment schedule.

The first payment may be on time; beware what follows. When you borrow from a bank, you sign a contract or open a line of credit. When you use your credit card, you can make minimal payments, but they won't get anyone to the finish line.

When a family member borrows from you, what regular payment plan will you negotiate? It's a given the loan will be interest-free (in most cases—perhaps) because that way you are helping your (insert name here) by saving them money.

How will you get your money if you lend it in good faith, but that member finds excuses not to hold up their end of the bargain? What will you do? Do you have a plan? Given that this is not the first time they've taken you to the cleaners, but they need the money and soft-hearted you, caved? Again. How will you handle such a situation? Discuss your expectations of lending money early in your relationship, stressing a firm payment plan is mandatory. And good luck.

It is best to come into the blended family with every scenario ironed out and agreed upon or as close as possible with firm procedures. Of course, no one in your family would dream of taking advantage of anyone in their home. Right?

COMMUNAL/SHARED AREAS

Entertaining family

EVERYONE WILL WANT TO attend special family celebrations like birthdays, school, graduations, or promotions, etc. With only one kitchen, preparations will be more difficult, especially if one person does the cooking in a small area. Another kitchen would make it easier, as would another pair of hands lighten the load. If the second kitchen allows more cooks, consider working together as a group if teamwork suits you or separately.

The more practical solution would be for everyone to bring a dish, especially those from outside the household. It's more fun sharing, anyway.

Entertaining friends

Grandma or Grandpa may not like the excitement the adults' entertaining causes and prefer to sit out some visits in their own space, be it in their room or the rec room or another space they occupy alone. They may choose to see a movie and leave altogether with their own plans. Do not take this as a negative. Too much noise is tiring and can be stressful, especially when vivacious children are in the mix.

Garden entertaining

How wonderful to provide the space for visiting family and friends to celebrate occasions in the back yard. When barbeque season arrives, it's prime time to take it outside. Less crowding, less cooking in a small kitchen, and less clean-up. A few salads and anything goes on the barbie. Fresh air and sunshine lift everyone's spirits and provide more elbow room and personal space. Have fun!

Smokers vs. non-smokers

Fewer people appear to smoke these days. Since small children are not used to smokers or other members of the family, are there rules for smokers in your house? Do you expect they take it outside? No smoking inside is a simple solution for everyone's benefit.

Kids, noise, and pets

No latchkey kids

WHILE ADULTS NEED TO work to keep the house running, children go to school unless they are toddlers or are homeschooled. Consider how wonderful for your child or children to be met at the door and given a drink and/or a snack after school instead of walking into a silent house, even if it's only for a couple of hours until an adult arrives home. The family pet, no matter how much the child loves it, will never replace a speaking, loving adult.

Homework help

If the children attend a regular school, grandparents are handy and know how to coax and supervise children's homework. Doing so before the household congregates for a lively supper removes the temptation to slide through homework when they're tired. Grandma/Grandpa don't rush and keep the children on track and may even make a game of it.

Children gain so much by interaction with the older generation. They lived interesting life experiences, even explaining how school and homework worked in the old days. The new math may confuse seniors if that is still in the school curriculum. Doubtless, grandparents can teach the kids real math, too. Can't hurt.

I can't help a giggle here as my first granddaughter—a fourth or fifth grader—explained the new math to me to no success. At her end, she thought the real math strange. Imagine that.

Homeschooling

Who has taken on this approach to educating your children? If Mom is the teacher, she might need a break. Grandparents are fountains of information and experience not found in the regular school core curriculum. Are they looking for something to do each day? There is more to schooling than reading, writing, and arithmetic. The seniors in your house are capable of some razzle-dazzle and can wow the kids with fabulous stories of life in the old days.

Countless resources and opportunities are obtainable for homeschooling. Do an internet search and you'll find oodles of information from your local school district with ready curriculum packages to buy (even free ones) from kindergarten to Grade 12. You will find free apps, websites, and live online classes. Materials and curriculum are available online, from Montessori among other organizations, and you can even build your own course of study. You know your child's strengths, weaknesses, and special interests best.

Find a homeschooling community for your own support online or face-to-face. The sky is the limit with what you can provide your children: others with like interests, playdates, variety of museum/park/touring trips of as well as occasions to form friendships.

Check laws and requirements in your country or state before you take on this project.

Noisy kids

Children aren't meant to be quiet or sit still. They're born to move, to run, and burn energy. Keeping them active outside in pleasant weather in a fenced yard is a win-win for everyone. The adults get a rest and the young ones will sleep like babies at the day's end.

Many were the days my young grandchildren had friends visit and ran across the hardwood floors above me with shoes on. Other times, they bounced hard balls on the floor. I had to leave the house when a headache developed. Earplugs did not work, and the visitors and their children were guests. Not I. (Discuss at the family meeting how to handle too-loud company.)

Teens are loud

If teenagers live with you, earplugs may become your best friends when ear-splitting music erupts from the living room. They like the music so much they want to live it, taste it, and feel it and this has nothing to do with being hard of hearing. You'd thought your hearing was going, well; it's really louder than you think it sounds. Smile and head for the hills.

Still, chances are a balance can be reached at a family meeting to respect the wishes of both the young and not so young.

Children and pets don't respect boundaries

Suppose you're in a crowded house with only your bedroom for privacy or noise relief. You lock the door for a reason. Children don't understand shut doors. When they want to see you, they come in.

If you live in the renovated garage, in the attic or basement, or even in a cottage in the backyard, don't expect curious children to understand closed doors. When they make their appearance, love the tykes, give them a moment of your attention, kiss and hug them before sending them on their way. You may only need to repeat yourself 10 or 20 times a day and miss your needed nap or endure several interruptions during a secret (think presents) or especially tricky project.

How many pets live with you? Pets don't respect boundaries either. Cats are known for their invisibility until they hear food dropped into their bowls. Other cats are in your face all day, sit or sleep in your favourite spot or chair, craving attention, fighting with the dog or not, scratching your furniture at will, jumping on the table when they smell food —your food—and the dog waiting for food to drop under the table. So, you either have cat hair on the table, on your plate or all over your pants from the chair the cat's wandered on. Surely this is a small price to pay for all the entertainment your four-legged creatures give you and the solace and comfort they give the children or you when you're not feeling well.

Too many pets: who cleans up?

If more than one owner has pets, who's on poop patrol. Who pays for the dog and cat food? What about the kitty litter? Who walks the dog(s)? Best of all, who gets to maintain the kitty litter stays fresh and smelling like a rose? What about vet bills? Shouldn't the pet owner be responsible for his pet's health and welfare? Aren't you glad they are yours?

So many things to discuss during a family meeting.

At our house, I still feed, water, and clean after the cats. I refuse to take on doggie duty as well. He doesn't belong to me as don't the cats other than my one. I took on the job to keep our home environment smelling clean because I am dependable. Pets are part of the family and deserve regular care. It's a win-win.

Respect the babysitter

Grandma and/or Grandpa love their grandchildren. It's their pleasure to see your little tykes grow and develop from little people to adults if there is time. Should aunts, uncles or cousins live with you instead, consider how thoughtless or unkind it is to expect them to babysit at the drop of a hat. Remember, chances are they made plans for the evening or during the week you wish to take advantage of for a quick getaway or a last-minute night out.

Retirement doesn't mean a rocking chair anymore. Life is for living for everyone in the household. Discuss and schedule nights out and babysitting so you don't put the other party at odds with one another's plans unless it's a matter of life or death.

A celebration after work may carry over to a neighbourhood pub even if you promise you'll stay for one drink, so making that phone call home won't matter. It matters since such thoughtless behaviour may interfere with the babysitting adult's plans. Teamwork and proper planning keep peace in the family.

What if one of the children gets sick and neither parent can be reached? Is your grandmother or grandfather babysitter prepared for that event? Do they drive? Where is the appropriate health coverage information kept should emergencies occur?

Disrespect of Property

Is it fair for one or more adults to leave dishes for someone else to pick up, leave boots or shoes in the way instead of on the boot rack or in the closet? Do you leave coats or scarves on chairs instead of hung in the closet? Do you clean up after your own children or pets when they make a mess? Do you leave a messy, cluttered bathroom after your shower?

Children are one thing. They don't know or understand the niceties, nuances, or thoughtfulness where other people are involved. You are no longer the child living at home being looked after by your parents. You are the parents. Show respect not only to the older generation but to all occupants in the home and give a better example to the children living with you.

When do we see each other?

WE BELIEVE EVERYONE DESERVES time for themselves and because privacy is such a premium, it is harder to attain.

We like our space and time alone as husband, wife, and children. Once in a while, we need to catch our breath and don't need to rub shoulders with everyone all day long. It's hard always pointing out and separating our individual space and cannot imagine spending time with extended members other than at weekly Sunday night dinners. You have your own lives to live, too. Life is busy, overwhelming, stressful.

Autonomy

Is there such a thing as spending too much time together? In a word, yes. Privacy is not just for the young. Spending days with active or hyper grandchildren tires you out. You need a nap or just quiet time.

You all need time to acclimate to this newer, fast-paced living in a louder environment than you're used to. Happy as the seniors are to live with extended family and the unpredictable comings and goings of visitors, strangers moving in, distant family members camping out temporarily or never leaving, your lives are disruptive. You love each other dearly, but it's okay to see each other less now and again.

Butting in vs. butting out

Though the younger parents were once your children, they are adults now and earned the right to teach and rear their children the way they wish. The older generation thought one way and saw things in a different light. Times have changed. It's hard but butt out.

If young parents are in the midst of a falling out or are arguing, please do not butt in with advice. Pretend you are not within earshot. This, too, is hard but butt out. Please.

How do you keep your daughter/son from being the cream in an Oreo? Be careful not to use them as go-betweens when there are misunderstandings among you. The worst action any parent can take is to complain to their married son or daughter and push an opinion on them. Their spouse's relationship with the offending in-law deteriorates because three opinions—the husband's, the wife's, and the interfering in-law is one too many for the couple. Again, three into two doesn't go.

When things get dicey: fighting, bickering, or hollering, butt out. How do couples argue and pretend they own their privacy to carry on without letting the entire household in on their differences of opinion?

Arguments are a normal part of living together, as are differences of opinion. It's only one point of view, but wouldn't you agree life might be boring if we all agreed on everything? Young couples are entitled to privately blend their lives as they mutually choose unless serious abnormalities or abuse in their arguments are noticed by anyone.

If I was not sharing my living space, although separate, within hearing range of disgruntlement or disagreements of my daughter and her family, I was privy to them because I was within hearing range. If they lived across town as they had been before we made our plan, I would be as ignorant of any vibes between them as any parent living apart. I pretended complete deafness to what occurred on the floor above me. I swallowed my tongue a time or two to keep my lip zipped.

If I had an opinion, it was none of my business to say anything about how they planned their lives, tended to their children, meals, hours of meals, or table manners, their friends, the way they dressed their children, what extra-curricular activities I believed their children might benefit from or enjoy. Yes, butting out is hard to do.

Pitfalls:

- Short tempers and shorter memories
- Avoidance of each other in daily life
- Avoidance causes misunderstandings or resentment
- A poor example for children
- Stalemates and in-fighting in marriage
- Living together becomes impossible and hard on a marriage

Mom/Dad needs help (repairs, moving objects)

When we all live in one basic house, whether a one or two-floor plan with bedrooms upstairs, the family intermingles all day, especially when you share one kitchen. Should this be the case, helping the grandparents with lifting, moving, or repairs isn't a scheduling situation?

If the grandparents live in their own area with a kitchen in the basement, attic, garage, or a cottage in the backyard, you need to arrange a time to help as you're separated into different locations.

Whatever the case, make them a priority. After all, they are looking after the children while you work, probably help in the kitchen, run errands, clean up, and carry out any number of timesaving tasks you should not overlook. Now is the time to not leave the seniors on the back burner.

Constant borrowing of food or other supplies

Suppose you own two kitchens and one family comes to borrow items not once but on numerous occasions, with the excuse, the store is closed or will close soon or any other reasons? How many times is enough? How do you nip this habit in the bud?

Nobody minds sharing, right? The trouble is you may need that particular item for yourself as that's the reason you stocked it.

Negotiations: bruised egos, misunderstandings

Misunderstandings will happen. We are humans, after all. When many people live under the same roof, it's what we expect if bumping into each other after a bad day at work and privacy is at a premium. Because moods fluctuate, there are bound to be differences that affect individuals in varied ways.

Do you need to call a family meeting if there is an urgency or can the problem wait for discussion at the next scheduled meeting?

How to cut expenses when you can't

YOUR LIFE HAS BEEN good, but the unexpected happens. You're forced to make a hard choice you weren't expecting. You'll be surprised how much is in your power to change, though these decisions are the hardest you've ever made. Sometimes you need to bite the bullet whether for a long time or for a while till you ride out the storm.

What if?

Times are hard. Life is hard. Hanging on to your job in an uncertain economy is—hard! You may consider yourself lucky the boss kept you on for three days a week at work instead of five. Imagine your boss is cutting expenses, too. Still, with a smaller paycheck now, what can you do to make ends meet?

Pay bills on time

Take note of the high rates of interest charged on late or outstanding bills. When you were busy living the good life, maybe this detail slipped your consideration, but now that you're watching every penny, pay all bills on time.

Better yet, pay cash and lay off the credit card. This way, you know exactly what you're working with. Temptation is a devil. No more you'll pay it next month. Who knows what unexpected expenses might turn up? You don't want to sell yourself short by losing sleep over an unnecessary expenditure when belt-tightening.

You may notice how paying by cash makes you more aware of how much and what you're paying for, and it's harder to part with the cash. Using a credit card has little awareness attached to it. Have you noticed how easy it is to swipe and forget with no angst involved? The plastic relationship to spending hard-earned wages has a lot less emotion attached to it.

Also, if your credit was good and you were a spender, the credit company raised your limit and in your non-emotional connection to dollars, you'll be sucked into spending more.

Hit the sales aisles

No matter the times, why pay more than you must for anything, anytime? Pat yourself on the back for every 'deal' you find.

No one should eat bad fruits or vegetables, but ugly fruit is only malformed and as edible as its perfect cousin, only cheaper. Other grocery specials are a wonderful opportunity to pick something to your liking at less cost, but you must watch everyday prices to make sure you are truly getting a bargain.

Hit the clearance and discontinued items section. If something has a dent or a scratch don't be afraid to talk to the manager to negotiate a discount. It's surprising how often this works in your favour.

Cut the cable

Cable is expensive and these days, what is worth watching at the high cost instead of streaming services the likes of Netflix or a mitt-full of other choices? Do you really watch enough for the cost? Just think about what is worth more to you, cable or a roof over your head and food on the table.

Public transportation

If you own a car and now drive it part-time to match your shortened work schedule, consider how much gas, maintenance, and car insurance cost. Compare public transportation vs. keeping your car and you'll be surprised how much you'll save.

If you must keep your car, map all your trips at once to save on gas and time.

Share with a roomie

Independence rules but sometimes it's better to share your space. Apartments are not cheap, but you might luck out and make a wonderful new friend and halve your housing expense if you're willing to share.

The payoff

Cutting back may not be fun at first, but once you get the knack, you'll wonder why you hadn't tried it before. How many new ways can you hatch to save even more than you ever thought possible? Think of it as a game where the winner is you.

Do it yourself

Instead of takeout, why not cook meals at home? Not only do you control salt but also the spices in your food, especially if you like food hot or not. Even if you're not an experienced cook, it is possible to savour a scrumptious meal if you do it yourself. Think of this as an olfactory adventure where magic can happen to tickle those salivatory glands. Experimenting in the kitchen is recommended for best results.

Try these:

Ramen noodles

Tired of Ramen soup even if you add a handful of peas or carrots?

Cook the noodles but don't break them up and drain well.

Add a little oil to your fry pan, dump in the noodles and about ½ of the seasoning package or a bit at a time not to overdo (any flavour on hand) and stir. Yum.

It's ready. Also, you can crack an egg into the pan and voilà. Double yum.

Spaghetti

Cook the noodles al dente.

While they're cooking, grate a clove or two of garlic (as much as you like).

Drain well when done. Toss a teaspoon of butter and a splash of oil or just oil into a fry pan.

Throw in the garlic till aromatic and add the spaghetti.

Mix well. If you've parmesan, sprinkle liberally but it will still be delicious without.

For more variety, add a favourite sauce, if handy.

Egg salad
Cook eggs and cool in cold or ice water. Peel and mash.

Add mustard and mayonnaise till creamy. Season to taste.

Any chopped onion? Add if you like.

For more variation, try relish, chopped pickle, chopped celery, or whatever you fancy.

Tuna salad
Drain the tuna and flake it with a fork. Add mayonnaise till creamy. Yum.

Consider adding chopped onion or garlic, chopped pickle or celery for variety.

Easy and delicious.

I HOPE THESE IDEAS have been helpful suggestions and paved a smoother understanding and transition for you and your family. I wish I had been more aware when I made the step forward. As I write this, I am still in an intergenerational home.

Thanks so much for reading.

About Author

Teresa Karlinski lives in Hannon, Ontario, in an intergenerational household with her cat Lady Gaga. A poodle named Max and four other cats belong to her daughter Laura and two granddaughters. Teresa enjoys reading, cooking, and writing nonfiction on occasion, but primarily writes contemporary fiction. She has been published in many anthologies. In July 2021, she translated and published a short memoir by her mother titled "Twist of Fate."

Teresa Karlinski
Contact me: teresakarlinski@gmail.com

Previously:

An Intergenerational Household Survival Guide: 1
Look Before You Leap
MINE, Ours and Yours

Coming soon:

An Intergenerational Household Survival Guide: 3
What Can Go Wrong?
Mine, Ours and YOURS

Printed in Great Britain
by Amazon

82055319R00036